AF407450

GROWING MINDS
BOOKS

I LOVE HOW

Dr. Isaiah Varisano

I love
how

you explore
new things.

I love
how

you practice
patience and
kindness.

I love
how

you share your
toys.

I love
how

you create new
things.

I love
how

you are willing
to help.

I love
how

you are
determined to
learn.

I love
how

when you fall
down you get
back up.

I love
how

you work hard
to solve
problems.

I love
how

you are willing
to try new
things.

I love
how

you keep
practicing to
improve.

I love
how

you don't give
up.

I love

you.

About Growth Mindset Praise

Growth mindset praise is a concept rooted in the work of Dr. Carol Dweck. Growth mindset praise refers to the practice of providing positive feedback and encouragement that fosters a growth mindset. A growth mindset is the belief that abilities and intelligence are not fixed traits but can be developed and improved over time through effort, learning, and perseverance. Growth mindset praise emphasizes the process, effort, and strategies used to achieve a goal rather than solely focusing on innate talent or abilities. Growth mindset praise puts emphasis on effort, encourages learning from mistakes, fosters resilience, motivates continued effort, and promotes a love of learning.

Tips for Growth Mindset Praise

1. Praise effort and perseverance, rather than innate abilities.
2. Encourage your child to embrace challenges and view failures as opportunities to learn.
3. Use language that includes the word "yet" to emphasize that improvement is possible. For example, "You haven't figured out how to do it yet, but we can practice".
4. Discuss the process of learning and how skills develop over time.
5. Help children set specific, achievable goals and break them into smaller steps.
6. Provide constructive, specific feedback on what they did well and what they can improve.
7. Avoid comparing children to others and focus on their individual progress.
8. Model a growth mindset by showing your own enthusiasm for learning and resilience in the face of challenges.
9. Create an environment that fosters curiosity and a love for learning.
10. Be patient and supportive, as developing a growth mindset takes time.